1 | PayPal Dispute Resolution

Disclaimer: Nothing herein shall be considered business, legal, or financial advice. The publication of this is for information purposes only and the content in it comes from personal experiences and it is not by any means business, legal or financial advice. Information may not be updated nor correct. I make no implicit nor explicit representation in regards to the information contained herein.

This book contains some Argumentation Techniques and Terms and Conditions suggestions or examples. These suggestions or examples are not by any means legal advice. You must address a licensed lawyer to get professional and legal advice on how to draft your T&Cs, draft an argument, and their legal implications.

Copyright © by Adriana Ubeda Martínez

ISBN: 9798544511557

All rights reserved. No part of this publication may be reproduced, distributed, or transmitted in any form or by any means, including photocopying, recording, or other electronic or mechanical methods, without the prior written permission of the publisher, except in the case of brief quotations embodied in critical reviews and certain other noncommercial uses permitted by copyright law. For permission requests, write to the author.

Foreword

Handling a dispute is not something you should take lightly as it can make you lose money due to malpractice, which can be avoided by reading this book. A dispute has to be won before it is opened by the Customer, meaning you should not take a passive approach and think ahead, pathing the way before a case is brought.

Having clear and strong terms and conditions on your site, notices, understanding how the platform where the dispute is brought works and its relevant T&Cs, providing relevant proof and arguments, and good previous communication with the Customer can surely increase your odds of winning the dispute.

This book will provide:

- Share of personal professional experience when handling disputes.
- Ways and practices to prevent a dispute.
- Language to improve or add to your terms and conditions.
- Explanation of the reasons why Customers can open Disputes (item not received, item significantly not as described, unauthorized transaction), what they consist of pursuant to PayPal T&C, ways to prevent them, etc.
- Acknowledgment of relevant PayPal T&Cs that can help you win the most common and usual cases.

- Claim Response Template Examples for each dispute reason.
- How to Respond to the Claim.
- Appeal PayPal resolution.
- Customer Service Precautions to path the way in case of a dispute.

Introduction

You (or the person in charge of handling disputes) don't need to be a lawyer, or understand the laws to win a dispute, but it is recommended that learn or know how to respond to claims in a lawyer-like manner because at the end of the day this dispute is just like a lawsuit but at a much lower level (no lawyers required to represent you), so it is important to know how to argue, analize, use the correct words, collect relevant evidence, have strong terms and conditions, etc.

It is also important to acknowledge the relevant terms set by PayPal on what constitutes "Item significantly not as described", "Unauthorized Transaction", "Item Not received". This book will not be filled with the boring part of PayPal terms and conditions as this book is not about their T&Cs, but I will make reference to them only when needed, as when drafting your dispute/claim you must base your arguments based on the rules set by PayPal.

I have had the opportunity to handle Disputes - on PayPal and other platforms such as Stripe - as a Dispute Resolution Specialist, as a Customer Service Agent who also handles Disputes, in different industries, and as a Business Owner as well who during the course of business has had the opportunity to be advised by a lawyer. This has allowed me to improve and to realize that when responding to disputes/claims on PayPal or Stripe even well-established companies make mistakes in the way they approach it. This leads the case being decided in favor of the customer, when it could have had a different result if handled differently.

There are, of course, particularities when handling a dispute on PayPal in comparison to a legal procedure. One of the main differences is that in theory, in a lawsuit or claim brought to a legal court the claimer or the person filing the lawsuit has the duty and obligation to provide proof of what she/he is claiming, and if you don't reply to the claim/lawsuit it will not mean that the defendant has lost the case because the judge has the obligation to confirm that the plaintiff has provided enough proof to support his arguments.

On the other hand, in PayPal if the buyer opens a claim, they usually don't provide any type of proof, and PayPal seems to take the Buyer's side, so if you do not respond to the claim, PayPal expressly says that they will rule in favour of the Buyer. So do not go ahead and think that you don't need to provide proof or don't need to reply to a PayPal claim because you think the Buyer's arguments are weak or that the Buyer has not provided enough proof.

The Customer can open a Claim/Case on PayPal by just saying she/he did not receive the product, and PayPal will transfer the burden of proof (duty to prove and to provide proof) to you. There are scenarios, depending on your business model or picked shipping carrier, where the tracking will not update (a very common issue faced by companies that export directly from China to the Customer where picking a cheaper shipping carrier can help you reduce cost but the problem with this shipping election is that the tracking will not update to the latest event and can be delivered without showing, just to name an example) and the only way for you to prove that the parcel was delivered is through the tracking update shown on the official national post office (USPS, Deutsche Post, La Poste, etc) but that is a proof you are not able to produce, hence your chances of winning the case are reduced, and increase the chances of Customer who know this loophole engaging in fraudulent activities opening claims on PayPal falsely claiming a product was not received but when in reality they did receive it.

It is also recommended that your business model reduces the chances of being subject to claims on PayPal because a while ago PayPal started charging a fee based on claims that escalate to Disputes from sales threshold, and the more claims you receive within a year, the higher the fee they charge you.

The content herein will try to address as much as possible what to be aware of in the different scenarios that might come up.

Chapter I

General Introductory Recommendations

<u>Go straight to the point:</u> While responding to the disputes/claims, I would recommend you to go straight to the point and keep information/proof relevant.

Besides the fact that PayPal gives you a limited amount of characters to write your argument, you must draft it as relevant as possible because you do not want the reader to get lost reading irrelevant information. Arguments like "we won't do anything to betray our customer's trust", "other customers received their packages" lead you nowhere.

<u>Your arguments must also match the "claim reason" chosen by the Customer</u> (provided that the Customer picked the right reason of why she/he opened the claim). This will be further addressed in the sections below.

<u>Customer Service Agent should not behave as a Dispute Resolution Agent, and vice versa:</u> An usual mistake made by companies is approaching the Claim as if a Customer Service Agent is handling it. A dispute is synonymous with a "fight", so the idea is that you cannot reply to the Claim asking the Customer for mercy, because that will also make PayPal think that the Customer is right and that you must refund him/her.

I understand that some customers open a dispute because the item has exceeded the estimated delivery time, so in this case the Customer has the high hand, but instead of saying "please wait a few more days to receive your item, most customers have been receiving their packages on time", saying "we understand the package has exceeded the estimated delivery time, but our terms and conditions state that there might be delays for reasons out of control such as weather conditions, custom clearance procedure, higher online purchase volume because of holiday seasons, less customs and airline personnel because of the covid-19 situation, and less flight availability, the Customer has not received the parcel but because of the aforementioned this purchase is not yet eligible for refund" can increase your chances of winning the case.

In the situation of the paragraph above, it is also recommended not to rush, and wait until a couple of days before the given deadline given by PayPal to respond to the claim if you think that the package will arrive before the deadline.

<u>Pick your fights:</u> there are cases where the Customer is totally right. If you, for example, send your packages from China, and not using any express shipping like DHL, UPS, etc, there is a chance that some packages will not be delivered, get lost, be sent back to the sender/warehouse, etc. If you have a 3 weeks

estimated delivery time, and the Customer has been waiting for 3 months or more, and opens a Claim, I would just refund the Customer or propose an alternative solution, i.e. give them the option to send it again but they have to close the claim first.

Propose an alternative solution: sometimes the Customer may be right and/or still want to receive the product instead of receiving a refund, and you might have a solution.

Maybe from a business perspective, and depending on your specific business model, it might come off cheaper and better to resend the product than giving a full refund.

Partial refund: You have to check the Customer's email or contact history to assess if the Customer is open to receiving a partial refund, this should be done only if the reason of the claim is because the "item is not as described" but it is still fully functional, or arrived damaged but there can still be given a functional use to it.

Offer the Customer to wait a few more days before deciding to refund or send it again: there are Customers that can understand that there can be delays due to reasons out of your hands, because of that they might be willing to wait a few more days or a couple of weeks, and if it doesn't arrive they can accept that you send a new item to them. You can also show them a sign of good faith by offering to issue a refund for a certain amount of the total price while they wait for the first package to arrive, i.e.10%, and either (1) issuing the total refund after the time to wait has passed, or (2) give the option to send the package again, only if this option (10% refund and sending it again) can help you mitigate your losses.

In those scenarios you have to tell the Customer that even by issuing a partial refund it is a loss for your business, and to kindly accept a partial refund to mitigate losses.

Propose to issue a refund but Customer has to send the item back to Seller: In the following 2 paragraph I will quote in Italic what PayPal has to say in regards to a settlement where Customer sends the product back to Sender in order to get a refund:

PayPal's original determination is considered final, but you may be able to file an appeal of the decision with PayPal if you have new or compelling information not available at the time of the original determination or you believe there was an error in the decision-making process.

IMPORTANT: You may be required to return the item to the seller or other party we specify as part of the settlement of your claim. PayPal's Purchase Protection program does not entitle you to coverage for the return shipping costs that you may incur.

Recommendation: because of the above, having the following terms and conditions will help you when requesting a settlement where Buyer has to send the item back to Sender in order to get a refund:

Example on what to include in your terms and conditions: If you open a dispute with a payment gateway service provider such as PayPal and/or Stripe because you claim the item is Not as Described, in order to get a refund based on the argument that item is not as described, you agree to send the items received back to sender at your expense prior to getting a refund.

Contact the Customer through the Customer Service Agent: it is true that what I have called "irrelevant arguments" above can help you make the Customer close the Claim by calling to the Customer Conscience, but such call has to be through the Customer Service Agent so you avoid PayPal taking this call to conscience as admitting that the Customer is right. Such a call to conscience has to be without admitting much guilt because this can backfire, and the Customer will use this "email" as a proof that he/she is right.

Dispute Resolution Agent must know about your business: Some businesses will have their customer support agents handling the disputes and others will hire another member to be in charge of them. Both options are valid, but in case you opt to have a different/new member handling the disputes, you must make sure that the Dispute Resolution Agent knows about your business, including business model, and has access to the support email/platform where the Dispute Agent gets to see the customers' tickets. All the mentioned above will help your agent to deliver a better response to the claim.

<u>Strong Terms and Conditions:</u> The Terms and Conditions will act as the Law equivalent. These terms will prove what the Customer agreed to when placing the order, no different from a contract. It is important to have these Terms visible before paying, like below the Pay button, and have the notice 'By placing this order you fully agree to our Terms and Conditions", with the link to these Terms.

If you have an automated system and you send emails (through an email campaign) to your customers, include a link to the terms and conditions of your company and always include an option where they can contact you.

When responding to these claims, complying with this recommendation will allow you to make arguments such as "our terms and Conditions clearly state that [there could be delays related to customs clearance], and the Customer agreed to our Terms and Conditions by placing the order, which is shown to the Customer before placing the order, please see the screenshot attached".

Following that recommendation will also allow you to attach the screenshot of where is the notice shown, and where are the terms and conditions shown, as a proof

The above will not allow the Customer to claim that she/he did not know the terms and conditions, or that the Customer did not see them.

Difference between Dispute, Claim, Chargeback and Bank Reversal

Now we'll talk about the difference between disputes, claims, chargeback and bank reversal. To do this I'll quote literally in italic what PayPal says:

Dispute/claim: *Buyer contacts the seller directly through PayPal's Resolution Center site to file a dispute, and the two parties work together to find a solution. If buyer and seller can't agree to a solution, buyer can escalate the dispute to a claim in order to request a refund/reversal where PayPal steps in to determine how the situation should be resolved.*

So we can conclude that a Dispute is when the Buyer initially contacts PayPal and tells them that there has been a problem with the purchase, and PayPal puts the money on hold. The Buyer has the option to discuss this matter with the Seller, or to escalate the Dispute to a Claim anytime before a certain date.

When the Buyer escalates the Dispute to a Claim, PayPal will intervene to make a decision on who is right, and might charge a fee as explained below.

What is the PayPal Dispute Fee and why was I charged one?

PayPal charges a Dispute Fee to manage the dispute resolution process on transactions that were completed by a buyer with a PayPal account or a buyer using PayPal Checkout as a Guest. This Dispute Fee applies to such transactions both when the buyer files a claim directly with PayPal and when they file through a chargeback with their card issuer or a reversal with their bank. The Dispute Fee does not apply to transactions processed through PayPal Pro or Advanced credit and debit card processing, sometimes called "unbranded" transactions.

The amount of the Dispute Fee depends on the percentage of claims filed against your total sales in the previous 3 months. The Standard Dispute Fee will apply unless your disputes rate is 1.5% or more and you had more than 100 sales transactions in the previous three full months. If you fall into that category, the High Volume Dispute Fee would apply for each dispute.

The Standard Dispute Fee will be waived for Inquiries in the PayPal Resolution Center that aren't escalated to a claim, those that are resolved amicably between the buyer and the seller, or those filed to PayPal directly as an Unauthorized transaction.

If a seller had more than 100 sales transactions in the previous three full months and their dispute rate over that time was 1.5% or more, they will be charged the High Volume Dispute Fee for each dispute. Otherwise, the Standard Dispute Fee will be applicable for each dispute.

Chargeback: Buyer contacts their card issuer and requests a refund.

PayPal states the following in its terms and conditions:

Your buyer pursues a chargeback related to a card-funded transaction and the transaction is not eligible for PayPal's Seller Protection program. The card issuer, not PayPal, determines whether a buyer is successful when they pursue a chargeback related to a card-funded transaction.

Bank reversal: *Buyer contacts their bank to request a refund.*

The above confirms that a chargeback or bank reversal is when the Buyer instead of opening a claim on PayPal opens the dispute through his/her banking institution, and then PayPal requires you to provide proof so it can be presented to the Bank on your behalf.

What's the difference between a dispute and a claim?

What is a dispute?

A buyer can file a dispute in the Resolution Center within 180 days of purchase if the item ordered doesn't arrive or is significantly different from the seller's item description. The buyer will be able to communicate the issue with the seller on a message board within the case. For example, the buyer can request a refund, return the item, and/or ask the seller to re-ship the item.

The seller will be notified of the dispute, and they should respond to the dispute and actively resolve the problem with the buyer. If the seller issues a full refund through the case, the case will be closed automatically. The buyer can also mark the case as resolved anytime if the issue is resolved to their satisfaction.

With a dispute, PayPal doesn't get involved or decide the outcome. To ask PayPal to step in, the case must be escalated to a claim within 20 days.

What is a claim?

If the buyer and seller can't reach an agreement on a dispute, either of them can escalate the dispute to a claim any time within 20 days of the date the dispute was opened. By escalating a dispute to a claim, they're asking PayPal to investigate the case and decide the outcome based on evidence supplied by the both parties.

A dispute that is not escalated to a claim within 20 days will close automatically.

Ways to prevent a dispute

There might be different options to avoid disputes by just providing good customer service and having good business practices. This does not mean that you will not find problematic customers along the way even if you do your best to provide an exceptional service to your customers.

Easy and open to Contact: The first and easiest advice that I can give you is to have good communication with your customers. I know that the communication can be affected by the size of your business but this simple step can prevent disputes.

Another way to prevent disputes is to assure and remind your customers that they can contact you at any time, and I suggest you to have your contact information visible on your social media pages or the website/platform where the customer made the purchase. If your customer does not see any contact information they will contact you for sure through PayPal.

If you receive a new dispute from a Customer that your support team have never been in touch with, I suggest you to contact the customer through email so you can let them know that you are willing to help or clarify any doubt regarding their purchases.

Keep it simple: Do not complicate the order process for your customers. Avoid having misleading information about the terms and/or prices of your products. This would save you more issues than you think, and also the support team would spend less time clarifying concerns which leads your company to better profits, a win/win situation 😉

It is true that sometimes some business and marketing practices can result in more sales, meaning more money for your business, which at the end of the day is the main goal for your company, (besides making your customers happy and creating a good relationship with them) but such practices may result in a higher dispute rate.

Also, be careful with hidden or recurring payments, such as subscriptions. If you do not warn your customers about them do not expect to win a lot of disputes for "unauthorized transactions".

Win your customer's trust. The more transparent you are with your business the better it would be for your business/company.

Keep an eye on the order status of the customers that complain very much or you think are prone to opening a dispute, but do not underestimate the ones that never contacted you. I have noticed that some customers would open a dispute before reaching out to the company customer service, which makes the process more difficult. If you see that their order is delayed, contacting them before they contact you will make your company look more professional and trustable, and this will prevent them from opening a dispute and more prone to accepting an alternative solution if the order is never delivered or if there is another type of problem with the package!

PayPal Non-Official and Official Dispute Resolution Process rules.

These are the non-official dispute/claim/appeal procedure rules (the rules explained on my own words):

- Buyer can open a dispute within 180 days after the date Buyer made the payment.
- Once a dispute is opened (the first step to initiate the process), PayPal will hold or freeze the funds while it investigates the case and until it closes the case and reverses the funds back to you, or issues a refund to the Customer.
- There are several possible outcomes based on the actions of each party. If a Customer opens a Dispute and you don't reply to the dispute, it will make PayPal automatically issue a refund to the Customer, but if you reply to the dispute and the Customer does not reply back to your reply nor escalates the Dispute to a Claim then PayPal will close the case and send the money back to you.
- If the Customer opens a Dispute, the Customer must scale it to a Claim before a given date; if the Customer doesn't scale it, the Dispute will be closed automatically. If you don't reply to the dispute before the given date, the case will be closed and decided in favour of the customer.
- If you don't reply to the Claim (a Dispute that has been escalated) before a given date, PayPal

will decide the case in favour of the Customer, even if the Customer did not provide any proof nor logic argument.
- A claim can be opened without first opening a dispute.
- You can appeal the claim decision within 10 days after the dispute has been decided for the first time.

Paypal Official Dispute Resolution Process rules.

To compliment my explanation above of the PayPal Terms and Conditions, they officially state the following in their T&C in regards to the "Dispute Resolution Process", quoted literally in italic:

Our online dispute resolution process.

If you're unable to resolve a transaction related issue directly with a seller, you must follow our online dispute resolution process through the Resolution Center to pursue a claim under our Purchase Protection program.

You may also file a claim (Step 2 below) by calling us and speaking to an agent. The steps you must follow are described below, and if you do not follow these steps your claim may be denied:

Step 1: Open a dispute within 180 days of the date you made the payment. This might allow you to start a direct conversation with the seller regarding your issue with the transaction that may help resolve the dispute. If you are unable to resolve the dispute directly with the seller, proceed to Step 2. We will place a hold on all funds related to the transaction in the seller's PayPal account until the dispute is resolved or closed.

Step 2: Escalate the dispute to a claim for reimbursement within 20 days after opening the dispute, if you and the seller are unable to come to an agreement, or we will automatically close the dispute. You can escalate the dispute to a claim for reimbursement through the Resolution Center. The seller or PayPal may also escalate the dispute to a claim at this point. PayPal may ask you to wait at least 7 days from the transaction date to escalate the dispute.

Step 3: Respond to PayPal's requests for documentation or other information, after you, the seller or PayPal escalates your dispute to a claim for reimbursement. PayPal may require you to provide receipts, third-party evaluations, police reports or other documents that PayPal specifies. You must respond to these requests in a timely manner as requested in our correspondence with you.

Step 4: Comply with PayPal's shipping requests in a timely manner, if you're filing a Significantly Not as Described claim. PayPal may require you, at your expense, to ship the item back to the seller, to PayPal or to a third party (which will be specified by PayPal) and to provide proof of delivery.

Proof of delivery means:

For transactions that total less than $750 U.S. dollars (or the currency threshold in the table below), confirmation that can be viewed online and includes the delivery address showing at least city/state or zip code, delivery date, and the identity of the shipping company you used.

For transactions that total $750 U.S. dollars (or the currency threshold in the table below) or more, you must provide signature confirmation of delivery. If the transaction is in a currency not listed in the table, then signature confirmation is required when the payment exceeds the equivalent of $750 U.S dollars at the PayPal exchange rate that applies at the time the transaction is processed.

Chapter II

The most common reasons for disputes

When a person is opening a claim, PayPal make them pick between one of the following three options:

- Unauthorized Transaction
- Item not received
- Significantly Not As Described

Unauthorized transaction:

Common Reasons Argued by the Customer in this scenario:

- You took the money without their consent (common scenario when the Customer has a subscription).
- Someone else made the purchase without the Account Owner Knowledge and/or Consent.

What is an Unauthorized Transaction?

An "Unauthorized Transaction" occurs when money is sent from the Customer's PayPal account that

Customer did not authorize and that did not benefit the Customer. For example, if someone steals your password, uses the password to access your PayPal account, and sends a payment from your PayPal account, an Unauthorized Transaction has occurred.

According to PayPal, the following are NOT considered Unauthorized Transactions:

If the account owner gives someone access to its PayPal account (by giving them their login information) and they use the account owner's PayPal account without Account Owner knowledge or permission. The Account Owner is responsible for transactions made in this situation.

Invalidation and reversal of a payment as a result of the actions described under Refunds, Reversals and Chargebacks.

Real Life example of what does not constitute an Unauthorized Transaction:

One time we received an order from a Customer, and in the order form the Addressee was the same person who owned the PayPal Account.

This person, about a week later, opened a dispute claiming that she did not authorize the transaction and that it was her husband who placed the order using her PayPal account without her knowledge/consent.

We argued that according to PayPal Terms, that transaction did not constitute an Unauthorized Transaction because (1) she gave her husband her login details, and (2) because the transaction benefited her because the order was placed under her name as the addressee.

The example above is very common, but in their excuse they just replace who was the relative who placed the order. They usually say it was their children, I guess to make it seem more credible.

Generalities:

This one is very common and this is usually from those customers who open the dispute/claim days after the transaction, or even wait months after receiving the package to open a dispute; I do not want to generalize, but this makes me suspect that the Customer might be engaging in fraudulent activities.

We often think that only the companies can be a scam, and that the customer gets the low end, but there are customers that use these illegal practices to order from online shops, get their products and then open a dispute for these purchases saying they did not authorize these transactions.

It is very likely that you can win these disputes, but you need to submit all the evidence needed to make you win, as well as writing a good argument.

Ways to Prevent a dispute for Unauthorized Transaction:

Terms and Conditions: you should add a language alike to the following to your terms and conditions:

Any order cancellation request shall be communicated or requested to the following email address "example@yourbusiness.com" within 24 hours after your purchase. We hold the right to deny, at our sole discretion, any cancellation request after the 24 hours time limit, this includes claimed unauthorized transactions.

Arguments that can help you win in these cases:

-You do not have access to the Customer's PayPal Login Details, and you cannot take money out of the Customer's account unilaterally.

-The Addressee of the Package is the owner of the PayPal account. If a third party made the purchase on behalf of the Claimer (the person / Customer who opened the dispute) because this third party had access to the account such as a relative, friend, or anyone else, that is a claim the Customer has to bring against this third party, and not your company/shop.

- PayPal granting this claim in favour of the Customer can allow this Customer and others to engage in potential fraudulent activities.

Relevant proof to be collected:

- Screenshot of terms and conditions.
- Screenshot of purchase receipt confirming the package is addressed to the Customer and to the Customer's address. Hence the receipt to be attached has to contain such information (addressee and address).
- Tracking number confirming the product has been shipped and/or delivered, so a refund is not possible as per your terms and conditions.
- If applicable, screenshot of the Customer asking to cancel the order after the 48 hours time limit set in the terms and conditions, or screenshot of any conversation where it is shown that the customer was aware of the purchase before she/he opened the claim i.e. emails asking when the package will arrive, email asking for the tracking number, or any other type of email that you think is relevant to prove that the customer was aware of the purchase.

Item not received:

Common arguments by the Customer:

- The item has not been delivered yet, either before the estimated delivery time has passed or not. They want the item or a refund.
- Tracking has not updated yet.

PayPal User Agreement states that Buyer will not qualify for a refund under PayPal's Purchase Protection program for an Item Not Received claim, if:

- Buyer collects the item in person, or arranges for it to be collected on your behalf, including if Buyer uses PayPal in a seller's physical store, except for in-person PayPal QR code goods and services transactions, or
- You, the seller, have provided proof of shipment or proof of delivery.
- If the You, the seller, present evidence that you delivered or shipped the goods to the Customer, PayPal may find the Claim in your favour, for an Item Not Received claim even if Buyer claims Buyer did not receive the goods.

Generalities:

Some customers receive their products but they still open a dispute saying they did not receive it. This is because the tracking information does not show that the package was delivered, so they know if they open a dispute claiming they did not receive their product, since it is difficult for you to collect proof that they indeed received it, they will get a refund.

It is worth noting that PayPal in some cases decides the claim in favour of the Customer even though the tracking information says it is delivered, and PayPal says the tracking link is not enough proof.

<u>Terms and Conditions to win this Claim:</u> you should add a language alike to your terms and conditions like the following:

Our estimated delivery time is XX business days. You acknowledge and agree that there might be delays for reasons out of our control such as less available flights, and less airport and customs personnel because of the Covid-19, and other factors such as weather conditions, epidemic, pandemics, disease outbreak, national holidays, strikes, etc.

It is the Customer's responsibility to make sure that the delivery address provided can be reached by the postal service, and that the mailing box has the size capacity to receive and store the package, and that the mailbox is in a secure location. We are not responsible for stolen packages because there was no secure location to deliver it or because the Postal Service was not able to reach the delivery location.

We highly recommend Customers to leave their phone number when placing the order so the Postal Service or Customs can contact you in case there is a problem with the delivery or customs clearance. We are not responsible for Customer's failure to promptly respond to a notice from either the Postal Service and/or Customs.

Relevant proof to be collected:
- Screenshot of terms and conditions.
- Photo of the shipping label where it is shown that the package was shipped to the Customer and to the Customer's Address. This shipping label should also show the product description, weight, etc.
- Screenshot of the order receipt, with all the order description included.
- Tracking number confirming the product has been shipped, and delivered if applicable.
- Any other relevant conversation with the customer that can prove the package was delivered, or any other relevant information as per the specific case.

Significantly Not As Described

Common Reasons Argued by the Customer:

- Order arrived Broken or incomplete.
- Item looks different from the one on the ad (size, color, etc).
- Item does not match the product description/features.

PayPal User Agreement states that an item may be considered Significantly Not as Described if:

- The item is materially different from the seller's description of it.
- You received a completely different item.
- The condition of the item was misrepresented. For example, the item was described as "new" but the item was used.
- The item was advertised as authentic but is not authentic (i.e. counterfeit).
- The item is missing major parts or features and those facts were not disclosed in the description of the item when you bought it.
- You purchased a certain number of items but didn't receive them all.
- The item was damaged during shipment.
- The item is unusable in its received state and was not disclosed as such.

Personal note: nothing stops a Customer from receiving the package with the complete order, and just taking a photo of half of the items (to attach it as a proof) and claiming they only received half of the ordered items. In this case, you can use the shipping label from the shipping company where it is shown the amount of items sent.

An item may not be considered Significantly Not as Described if:

- The defect in the item was correctly described by the seller in its description of the item.
- The item was properly described but you didn't want it after you received it.
- The item was properly described but did not meet your expectations.
- The item has minor scratches and was described as "used."

Type of Product You Sell

Your arguments will depend on the nature of the product you sell.

If it is a handcrafted, natural, artisan, art, or just a product that by its nature cannot be reproduced with the exact same outcome, and the customer claims it is not as described, you can argue this, and you also must have a visible notice saying that on the website so you can send a screenshot of this notice as a proof.

This does not mean that under that argument you will be entitled to send a much different, low quality, or defective product claiming that the product is natural, for example.

<u>Notice example to be displayed in the product page (this notice can also be added in the terms and conditions so you have an extra layer of protection):</u>

The photos are for reference only. The color of the product in the photo may be affected by your device color set up or setting, and the product size may be affected by the camera angle. Please check the product details to know the actual item description.

Relevant proof to be collected:

- Screenshot of the product details on the product page.
- Screenshot of the relevant parts of your terms and conditions.
- Shipping label where it is shown the amount of products sent.
- Screenshot of their order receipt to prove what the Customer ordered.

What if the Customer picks a reason for a claim which is different from the arguments in it?

Some customers don't know how to open disputes/claims, and this can be a point in your favour. For example, If a Customer receives an incomplete order, the Customer might intuitively but wrongly pick "Item Not Received", when according to PayPal T&Cs the correct pick is "Significantly not as described". In this case you should win the dispute by just providing proof of delivery.

In addition, some customers have not received their products and instead of choosing "item not received" they choose "Significantly Not As Described". You can win the dispute by claiming how is it possible that the Customer says the item is not as described if he/she has not received the item yet?

Keep in mind that the customer can change the reason for the claim once they feel trapped. You can make PayPal doubt her word by recalling that the Customer keeps changing the reason for the dispute/claim and that it should be a red flag for fraud.

Another example are those customers that received their products and then open a dispute/claim for "Significantly Not As Described" but they never detail and show proof for said claim. This can be good for you because you can use this in your favour when you are drafting the argument.

Chapter III

Responding to the claims

Language: I think communication during the dispute/claim should be in a passive-aggressive manner if you have grounds to win the case. Passive can mean being comprehensive with the customer, but yet be bold when drafting your arguments (not asking for mercy).

If the Customer is right or has more odds of winning the claim than you, you should adopt a constructive language seeking for a solution that benefits the two of you.

Picking the right reason to disagree with the Claim: PayPal gives you 3 or 4 options to respond to the claims depending on the reason chosen by the Customer who opened the Claim. Make sure to choose the reason that will match the arguments to be given and proof you will submit. If you don't know which option to pick, you can choose "I disagree with this claim".

Submitting evidence: it is highly important that you submit evidence when responding to the claim. This evidence should be relevant and match your arguments.

For example, if you respond to the Claim saying the package was delivered, the appropriate evidence would be providing the tracking number and the tracking information link from the official postal service (USPS Website, La Poste, Canada Post, Royal Mail, etc) or shipping line. It is also good to attach a photo of the shipping label so PayPal can confirm you are providing the correct tracking number.

You should also attach the order receipt where it is shown what the Customer ordered, and the shipping address, etc.

Terms and conditions: The terms and conditions need to be as detailed as possible.

The importance of having the terms and condition of your store displayed where appropriate will make sure that the Customer won't be able to claim that she/he was not aware of your T&C.

The terms and conditions suggestions in this book are just for specific sub-clauses examples. When drafting your terms and conditions you must get the help from a lawyer to foresee any possible scenario, and to make sure they are, if needed, GDPR and or CPRA compliant.

Appeal

If PayPal decides the case in favour of the Customer, you have the option to Appeal the outcome, but the Appeal button will only appear for a 10 days period. If the 10 days period has passed, you have the option to contact PayPal to see if you can Appeal.

When you appeal the case you must present new information.

For example: If the package is delivered after the PayPal decision but no later than 10 days after the decision, you can appeal the case with the new information, such as: Tracking number, screenshot that proves the delivery, the address given by the customer when placing the order, etc.

It is not recommended to Appeal if you are bringing the same arguments and proof from the initial claim. I understand that you may want to appeal a decision wanting a different person to consider your case or the decision, but PayPal says "Generally, the decision made at the conclusion of a claim is final and can only be appealed if new information is presented, which was not considered during the original review."

Nonetheless, nothing stops you from appealing to try and see if the decision is reversed even though you are bringing the same arguments.

Templates

Disclaimer: these templates are drafted as generic as possible to give you an idea of the language used when replying to a Claim. All cases are different and these templates must be modified accordingly.

Item not received/ Delivered

This order was delivered on June 1st, 2021 to the address she provided in the order form.

The address is: [insert the shipping address provided by the customer when placing the order]

The tracking number is: [insert tracking number]

[Insert National Postal Link or the Shipping Line confirming the delivery]

According to PayPal User Agreement, Buyer will not qualify for a refund under PayPal's Purchase Protection program for an Item Not Received claim, if Seller has provided proof of delivery.

For proof of delivery, it is enough the confirmation that can be viewed online and includes the delivery address showing at least city/state or zip code, delivery date, and the identity of the shipping company Seller used.

We have provided enough proof that the product was delivered by [USPS, Royal Mail, Canada Post, UPS, DHL,etc] because the official postal service website states so, and we also have proved that we mailed the package to the address the customer provided. If PayPal grants this claim in favour of the customer (name of customer), this would allow this customer and other customers to engage in fraudulent activities, allowing them to receive their products/orders, and then open claims to get their money back, leaving us sellers at their mercy.

Please see all the documents attached and links provided.

Appreciate your help investigating this matter. We are open to provide any further proof that you require.

Item Not Received

Not delivered yet

I disagree with this claim because our terms and conditions clearly state that there may be delays on our estimated delivery times because of the Covid-19 situation which leaves airports and customs with less personnel and less available flights, or other delays like customs clearance, weather conditions, etc.

Because of the above, this order does not meet our requirements for a refund. The Customer agreed to our terms and conditions when placing the order.

Please see the proof attached where it is shown our terms and conditions, and where they are shown to the Customer before and after placing the order.

You can also verify our terms by clicking on the following link: [insert link]

In addition, PayPal T&C state that Buyer will not qualify for a refund under PayPal's Purchase Protection program for an Item Not Received claim if the seller has provided proof of shipment.

The order is on its way to the Customer, and the order tracking number is: [insert tracking number]

You can verify the tracking number through the following link: [insert link]

Unauthorized transaction

I disagree with this claim as it does not qualify as an Unauthorized Transaction according to PayPal T&C because the Customer Login details were not stolen, hence the Customer is responsible for this transaction, and this transaction benefits her/him as it is addressed to the account owner [add customer full name]. Customer visited our store and placed the order, where she willingly added her shipping details, and also continued to log in to PayPal to make the final payment. The Customer is the only one who has access to her PayPal account, therefore any payment going out of her account was authorized by her, and if it was placed by another person, she shared her login details.

In addition, this transaction does not qualify for a refund under our terms and conditions because they state that any cancellation request shall be sent within 24 hours after the purchase, and this order has already been shipped. Please check the following link and the attached shipping label: [add link]

If PayPal grants this claim in favour of the customer [customer name] this would allow this customer and other customers to engage in fraudulent activities, allowing them to receive their products/orders, and then open claims to get their money back, leaving us sellers at their mercy.

Appreciate your help investigating this matter. We are open to provide any further proof that you require.

Note: if you lose the claim on PayPal, you have the option to appeal the decision, and give the customer the option to issue a refund in exchange of the Customer sending the package back to you (the Customer will have to bear the shipping expenses).

Item not as described

Customer did not elaborate why the item is not as described

Generic template: the customer did not elaborate the reason why the item is not as described:

If the customer opens a claim stating that the item that she received was not as described, she must first prove that the item that she received was indeed not as described. For such purpose, she could have sent a picture of the items so we (the company/store) and you (PayPal) could confirm that in fact, the item was not as described.

According to our EXCHANGES policy, we only replace items 5 days after delivery and this order was delivered months ago. So we cannot refund her and we do not accept the item back.

I attached a photo of our exchange policy.

Appreciate your help looking into this matter.

Item not as described

Looks bigger/smaller in the photo

I disagree with this claim because the product details clearly states the size of the item which is XX cm/in, and that the photo is for illustration purposes only as the item size and color perception can be influenced by the camera and item angles and the color set up of the Customer device.

Since the item was correctly described, it does not qualify as "Item not as described', even though the Customer claims it did not meet his/her expectations.

Please see the screenshot attached and the link to the product details where you can confirm the above information: [insert link]

According to our terms and conditions we can only issue a total or partial refund or resend a product if the product arrives damaged or incorrect.

Appreciate your rightness and solving this claim in adherence to PayPal T&C. We are open to provide any further proof that you require.

BONUS!!!!

Cancelled pre approved payment

(for recurring payments i.e. memberships)

I disagree with this claim because if the customer would have cancelled the subscription in the first place, she would have never been billed for the membership. We never received a cancelation email from this customer and he/she never canceled it directly with PayPal or with us before her/his billing date (her/his billing date is every Xth of the month). The order is on its way so we are not able to cancel and refund the order / The order is already delivered so we are not able to cancel and refund the order. Here is the tracking number XX

According to our Membership Terms and Conditions, Customer has to send an email requesting such cancellation before the billing date, and Customer has not provided proof to you that she/he sent this email request, nor the Customer cancelled the recurring payment directly with PayPal before the billing date. Please check the screenshot attached with the relevant terms and conditions, and the link to them: [insert the link to the T&Cs].

Appreciate your rightness and solving this claim in adherence to PayPal T&C. We are open to provide any further proof that you require.

Last words

I thank you for reading this book and I hope the content has helped you learn more or something about PayPal Disputes and Claims, which is the purpose of this book.

I tried writing this book in the easiest way possible, where I could share my experience and knowledge.

Please feel free to send me an email to share your thoughts and I would love to hear from you, your experience, or any constructive feedback :)

adriubeda25@gmail.com

The illustration/vector in the book cover is from Vecteezy.com.

The cover was designed and made by author.

www.ingramcontent.com/pod-product-compliance
Lightning Source LLC
Chambersburg PA
CBHW070858220526
45466CB00005B/2031